THE BOOK OF UNNAMED THINGS

Paul Hoover

a plume editions book

AN IMPRINT OF MADHAT PRESS

ASHEVILLE, NORTH CAROLINA

MadHat Press
MadHat Incorporated
PO Box 8364, Asheville, NC 28814

The Library of Congress has assigned
this edition a Control Number of
2017960763

ISBN 978-1-941196-60-1 (paperback)

Text by Paul Hoover
Cover image by Marc Vincenz
Cover design by Marc Vincenz

Plume Editions
an imprint of MadHat Press
www.MadHat-Press.com

First Printing

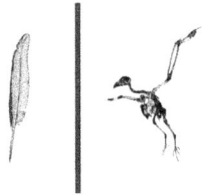

.

THE BOOK OF
UNNAMED THINGS

TABLE OF CONTENTS

Darkness of the Subjunctive

If it hadn't rained, we would've gone to the beach
—Phuc Tran

If we were in infinity, we would be everywhere,
even inside ourselves, as taste resides in the walnut,
and the walnut resides in the shell.
Then we would thrive inside the subjunctive,
where nothing happens but dreams of being,
as paradise dreams of its inferno,
the inferno of cotton candy.
If only the world had ripened, like a pear,
it might have melted the mirror in me,
delivering its softness to the hard road of the mind,
sixty miles from town.
      And if our grammar were even to our heat,
comma, conditional phrase, comma,
we'd be addicted to the sentence,
sentenced to an exile that sees, hears, and thinks,
and is often mistaken for love.
      Trees are chronologies;
every leaf shines, and in turning over it winks an eye:
if, if, and *then.* The world is possible meaning;
the world is possible, meaning:
I might have been an elf, had I been elfin.
But I am not an elf. I am a giant with tiny hands:
would, could, and *should.*
Had I been winged, I might have flown
from industrial field to pastoral alley
on great woolen wings, with the blue face of a bee.
Then it would have been said, "He is repairing to his persona"
or "He is retiring to his future."

I'll copy this by way of the stars, reflective.
Get back to me by facsimile or dream of climbing a night ladder
to the place of ideal size, near a town of simple affection.
If we had been born, lived our lives, and died,
we might have existed. On the side of darkness, infinity;
on the other, a sixty-watt bulb.

First Language

No time for the real; it's much too slow.
No time to peel a lettuce, no drudgery
of what is. It's all too familiar
when the neighbor's yellow flowers
bang their heads against the door.

The sky descends closer and closer;
the night defends the old orders. The real
is much too tragic. Fiction is the essence
on the gray road to magic. Thank you, yes;
thank you, no. No time for love, either;

there's too much falling. Everyone's
reeling from having so much feeling,
a burden and a prize, your mouth forever
singing and body parts swollen from
love's sheer labor, the years of smiling

for no good reason and all those nights
of crying. And then the families to visit
including those departed, a thousand postures
of doubt and knowledge, the well-dressed
window staring at the blank one, and oars

that float away. No time for life, either,
the world with all its sores, the daily grind
of subtleties and childhood triumphs.
Let the earth have it. A small song sung.
The train prepares distance, a station

rehearses staying. We can't help being
the person we impersonate, and now
another one's coming. No time for being;
it takes too much dying. The world
with all its doors and only one open.

But the new ordeals are over; the old
ones have begun. As shadows sway
on the sun-gray ground, we double speak
distance and the things it has to say, coinciding
with ourselves and our selves once more.

First language then the world, desire and
its words: *I got a bone to pick with you.*
The folded and enfolding, like what
we meant to say, with its sharps and flats.
Naked and disguised, the bodies we prepare.

Written

The written stone rests
in the unwritten river;
unwritten rain is falling
over the written town.

Nothing written today,
but tomorrow you'll be written
as you sit in your room not writing.

Lo, it is written.
Pollen writes on the stamen.
The man writes a child
in the body of the woman.
Your eyes write the view
into the window,
but it doesn't stay forever.
It returns with you into the unwritten.

All that means is written.
Lo, a tiger of a word
has escaped its cage.

Our quiet words
wait beneath the stair
for a reason to speak,
an edge or fold or cause
to remark. *Oh*, we say,
no way and *no how*.

This is how the world begins,
dark branches written
against a white sky.

The written stone rests
in the written river;
written rain falls
over the written town.

Handwritten

this is handwritten
    touched by no voice

hand and mind moving
    in search of a dwelling

a form of resurrection
    the language rich in spoor

something like infinity
    plus the number one

sensations aren't fictions
    distances reach your skin

become the world you're in
    the scent of lemon peel

reminds you of the real
    summerbread, heartleaf

serve as "groundation"
    not intrusions but the basis

meadow comes to mead
    mountain to its scree

night wears night-glasses
    feeling for its way

the deepest cut is absence
    its essences running in

forty-watt glamour
    of words upon the page

whose intentions are we
    call the night watchman

the pig from his pen
    our father in heaven

must have been dreaming
    impercipience please

not the gold standard
    eagles are not endless

and neither is resemblance
    a woman's green face

laughing in the painting
    matter, *mutter,* is only matter

it doesn't love or hate
    the bullet doesn't despise

the body it pierces
    it's only following orders

a hummingbird pierces the flower
    looks quickly into your eye

so busy it's hazy
    and where does it sleep

we are on our way
    never quite arriving

our words are only stations
    metaphysical weather

for an actual grammar
    summer seems to be slipping

back into the spring
    the shine on each leaf

knows what we're thinking
    it won't be long now

before all is known
    if not quite understood

squirrels fly
    birds swim

shadows don't lean
    their objects do

get out of paradise
    your pronoun knows

there's a sale on shoes
    at J.C. Penney

Dead Man Writing

The dead man smells of cigars and roses,
of turpentine and persimmons.
The dead man yells, but only the cat,
grown far too thin, and a lonely child
named Moises can hear him.

Erect in a kitchen chair,
in the place where he had lived,
his hand moves heavily over the page.
The boy hears him scratching
and thinks the cat wants in.

Soon he has filled a page,
then many pages, but he is not revived.
His writing fills one room then another.

The dead man is not distinct
from the shadow of his hand.
The stain of his pen is great.
We believe the world was created
in a similar fashion.

In most rooms,
there is light somewhere,
allowing a face to be seen
or the size of a dead man's shoe.
Light insists more than darkness;
it can awaken a room entirely.

A mouse also lives there,
chased all night by the cat.
They move like breath in a furious circle,
like the soft liquid of an eye
intent upon seeing.

The Book of Nothing

Nothing isn't empty.
It fills a room so completely
it spills into the street.
Everything comes from nothing.
Something, poor something,
stands vacant at the door.
A rose opens and opens
until its petals fall.
Then it seems vacant,
like a room with one chair.

Beauty is always fading.
We know an object best
when it starts to disappear.
Words are here but nothing,
meaningful sounds passing
then nothing but pleasure.
Light and space are something
passing through the trees.
A cry is heard in the distance.
It is something briefly
and then present absence.

A background seems like nothing
until a figure emerges, from what
seems the beginning.
But there is no beginning.
Something always comes before,
receding here, approaching there.
Only you remain

13

to bring it back from somewhere—
that shade of blue in the hallway,
black depths of the water.
Yellow fires, gray earth, and green
of wheat are something: actors
without equal, cock-crowing town.

Everything nature says
is ancient, careless, and cruel,
but it has no concept of nothing.
Leaning against a sunlit wall,
it projects casually something.
A mirror out of doors
catches the eye because
our eyes are in it, because
it seems to eye us
as part of its nature.

The overlord language resides
there, too: a stain, nerve knot,
with its incessant naming.
It comes into being, breathes,
then fades away again.
What was that? we ask.
Did you hear something?
It was nothing, says the cook.
A ghost, insists the chaplain.
It was dinner, says the hen,
so philosophical lately,
and always about one thing.

The Book of Unnamed Things

The house where he was born
fills with dust and birdsong.
Its rafters crash in memory.

She begs of the book of measure
a seam of restlessness and also
desperation. No title yet
for the book of names.

What to do with unnamed things
and the shadows they are cut from?
A sun for the book of origins,
moon for the book of sources.

He took the road of snow
to the house of exhaustion
where the book of ice was written
in the language of rain.

She sang in rain the ending
of a life too weary to speak.
The book of the sea was written
in the book of all that is.

He sang things into being,
recited the book of life
to a melon patch and dog days.

She was born and crawled sideways
toward a light she remembered.
She stands in the book of standing,
writes a page in the book of night,
sleeps one day and the everlasting.

He leans in the book of leaning.
Time, he knows, is on his side,
the vagrant house, wandering far,
hand of fire on the throat of fire,
the book of sand, its pages turning.

She unwrites what's before her,
keeps close what's gone away.
She asks the ceiling to oversee
what's spoken and what's silent,
a reason for the book of ending,
and just cause for beginning.

Why is Quiet "Kept"?

They are crying out in restaurants,
so delighted to be speaking,
they appear to be insane.

But we are the silent types,
who hold speech within
like the rustle of gold foil.

We eat our words and swallow hard.
There's nothing much to say.
The knot's in its nest, breathing.
A hand thinks it's a bird.

The world "nows"; it doesn't know.
The world "wows." Then it snows.

A word arrives, silent and upright.
It stands in profile against a white wall.
It's here for safekeeping only.

Keep quiet, mice.
A cat's patrolling the area,
with drones and more drones.

The keys we carry unlock us every day
and lock us up again. Hushed is the ward.
Now conjugate, please, *to werd* and *to werld.*

One of us has just conceived
the sum for infinity: plus one, plus one.
In the cosmological phone booth,
there's always one more.

The fishing report's too thick to read,
but its cadence is that of a god.
Waves and ships are passing.
We can barely discern the semaphores
flashing through the fog.

And here are the ones who walk the walk and talk the talk,
blackening the day with news, with news.

The Windows (Speech-Lit Islands)

as if for the first time
    you recognize the grass
        its greenness uncanny

in trying to be green
    as if for the first time
        you open a letter

that had fallen
    through the door
        its message unique to you

had you been
    as perhaps you seemed
        the neighbor

the one whose name was yours
    who finally joined the army
        had you in fact a country

a life to give
    wife and family
        as if for a while

you could read the signs
    remembered to unlearn
        how the wind feels exactly

going up your spine
    sensed the wheat sinking
        into the ground nearby

the whiteness of milk
    its mystical skirt uplifted
        miss meat and miss gravy

as if the language
    were smudged with words
        speech-lit islands

that don't submerge in meaning
    as if light itself
        were never in doubt

on the question
    of transcendence
        bees sing bells ring

in the ear's black window
    you whisper to the glass
        its past in sand

step back please
    a sentence is passing
        someone's calling

someone's raining
    door's creaking contradictions
        what bride is not disheveled

by all the world's scissors
    make-shape shiftings
        been a long time

since you wrote yourself in stone
    auto-lithographic
        [I] seems to be alone

[I] suffers in a crowd
    but not a yellow room
        in not a yellow town

everyone's on loan
    but someone here knows
        why nimble people cry

a bullet makes you die
    and then there's you
        absent sometimes laughing

as if at last
    there is no non-journey
        across the whole word

what are you thinking
    conjured of a god
        pears you'll never taste

lines not written
    what you know you are
        you'll never be again

The Urgency

The ghosts with names and the ghosts with none
—Michael Palmer

the tree in heat
the burning tree

the cat on fire
the urgency

shadow hat
hat worn flat

future-past
dust in advance

carry me home
beyond the bone

dolls on the bed
one playing dead

they are not,
and they are air

float on up
or take the stairs

minds are windows
winds have rows

the word false
is also true

kill me twice
shame on you

why the night
and light go under

speaking from
the heart's penumbra

standing tall
is not a science

what's a color
why's a sight

torrents, pools
a fool's forever

first the image
then the rain

light of science
scent of pears

the sun is raw
the moon is new

first the marriage
then the weather

push the car
and crash the carriage

hysterical cleric
untold tale

bearing witness
names are blameless

crucifixion or
a game of tennis

cross the valley
swim the ford

flesh has answered
bone's on hold

did we ever
when's undone

in Fargo, in
the Target store

Made to Resemble

a match is like a shard
the shard is like a sword

a sword is like a word
the house of water folds

the past is like a bowl
the future's like a rope

a rake is like resemblance
don't step on one oh no

mimesis is like mimesis
a tree is like a weed

a lie is like a fiction
a fiction's like a deed

a shoe is like a shape note
an eye is like an island

the goose is like the gander
the sandman's like the sand

a ribbon's like a stipend
the bend is like the road

the cross is like a crisis
hope is like a bone

the season's like a threshold
the forest is like a door

rats are like the righteous
the green are like the gold

life is like a sentence
a bird is like the world

reason is like erosion
names are like tin bells

to seek is to be looked for
to leap is like to fall

to think is to be distant
a soft spot's like a blow

a river's like a wellspring
the dead are like the soil

a chair is like a grandstand
the sky is like a dome

the sailor's like the wave
the night is like the day

the bride is like the groom
the grain is like the wood

the end is like the beginning
the cut is like the blood

Define: Mother Tongue

made of flesh or ink
you are not alone

restless at the door
she's part of the descent

into you and through
something traced

on transparent paper
a phantom limb

spoken back into being
and that prime witness

has long since disappeared
only the fiction lives

breathless as a fish
the future is seismic

its needle twitching
the possible appears

fugitive realm of
blossom, nightmare

compass, mole
each moment is a season

its memory scented
your mother sprouts wings

and flies into the sun
the planets stop turning

a red scarf flies
back into the present

Unspoken

words canter
draw together

into what is
called silence

in the pause
a weight falls

lends gravity
to your life

nothing missing
nothing gained

words unspoken
remain forever old

you're excited
to be exiled

to the place
of not speaking

the thought of
not thinking and

sea of not being
fold over as sound

Paul Hoover

take a breath
and you're sleeping

no ending
to the sound

of the world
unspeaking

Define: Contemplation

If they went beyond the husk,
the seed lay gleaming.

If they went beyond the flesh,
the bone lay pale.

They were eating the dialectic
and the marrow of difference.

They consumed abhorrence
and something Duns Scotus said.

They went beyond desire,
past "qualitative forms,"

a "tactics of resistance,"
and radical grammar.

They were eating ideas.
Space unfurled around them.

Time let down its gown.
Dominant systems of sense-making

had nothing left to say
but said it now and then.

Nothing was left to love,
but much could be declared:

abandonment of history,
the future passing away.

They were hungry for a moment,
but time would not comply.

They had eaten their ideas,
and dessert was still to come—

some kind of essence
with existence in its wings.

Chinese Figures

let me say the song
    that will sing it well

song's long sound:
    cries along the hall

hare in the moon
    man on the ground

the doors are wide open
    all is context now

•

no thatched cottage
    but a beach house on the hill

the rain is heavy
    mist all over the roads

cars driving slowly
    and in the wrong direction

no footsteps on the landing
    none in the house

a showplace for the sun
    everywhere it goes

hot on the water
    caught among the rocks

shining up the stairs
    the right way now

gods on the ground
    are changed by their desires

•

sounds like something real
    but no one spends attention

we're overloaded now
    every surface known

indecently as well
    a culture numbed and stung

by the image it's become
    work it hasn't done

everything's forever
    no changes in the sun

what feels old is triumph
    silence begs a hearing

something like a pause
    every note is yes

there's no such thing as none
    until you add it up

·

hold me in your hearts
    fold me on your tongues

fire's song, tree's gone
    now the lights are on

silly yet indecent
    innocent as well

syllables are able
    it's a tribal day

nature makes mistakes
    all of them ours

it knows what we have done
    before we have conceived it

dust falling modern
    on all the neighborhoods

time's up but keeps on raving
    as they drag it from the stage

      •

here we are, the world
    what is and what has been

how much dark is needed
    before we know it well

let me keep this keeping
    mu is wood, *quang* enclosed

enclose them with a bell
    soften it with snow

sleeping on the run
    dreaming of extinction

everyone sleeps alone
    on the ice of his choosing

we open the forest door
    and the light brims over

all dreamed things are open
    no knowledge of the closed

      •

the swallows dart quickly
    but the owl is heavy

people leave their porches
    to watch television

history will remember
    eternity came early

blue light in the windows
    as far as you can see

you don't feel much
    don't think much either

the little dog hates you
    even when it smiles

something in the language
    doesn't know us well

ten kinds of typeface
    and not one style

•

not exactly poignant
    the price of merchandise

guess we'll have to find
    another culture later

space is too exacting
    and time wears plaid

we have lived our lives
    according to its plan

Repetition and Difference

The infinite resources of the thickness of things
—Francis Ponge

swept snow and kept it.
    empty arms waving.
birds erased by wind.
    a journal of aesthetics.

a train is the ghost.
    slipping through the zoo.
the fog itself is warm.
    too primitive to be dreary.

cold mountain beings.
    wearing stone clothing.
the history of empty space.
    steaming at the table.

the modern world is tender.
    snow on all its owls.
to sing an empty room.
    go to bed scowling.

a sensuous apprehension.
    leaps the world's meanings.
what do you mean *boulders*.
    along the doorway border.

he called it diamond silence.
    hidden by its brightness.
river and its ladder.
    sun falling on your knees.

a roaring river fire.
    house key in the snow.
must be silence walking.
    in three-word groups.

comparable to water.
    a white trackless skyway.
dogs sleep on the road.
    beneath the sound of scree.

among the honey jumpers.
    bleary to the bone.
it's warm underground.
    her lovely snapping eyes.

the world's leaf laden.
    that's a yellow path.
handprint on the window.
    it's never egret season.

an oath before we sink.
    punching holes in water.
blue lupine eyes.
    and for a common cause.

eternity's going slow.
    about to take the corner.
who's immortal now?
    the stove's about to go.

another ragged actor.
    your permanent shadow.
naked in that realm.
    all laughter is solemn.

distance is in ribbons.
    don't hurry falling down.
it was called the lipstick riot.
    I heard strains of music.

the unaccountable stars.
    tell a public secret.
crayfish and momentum.
    sleeping isn't resting.

resemblance is a peach.
    the sunlight's whipping now.
a valley three states wide.
    and not a single fire.

a life of ledge walking.
    seems so normal now.
no tree falls inward.
    I'm your gun for hire.

the campfire takes a walk.
    across six mountains.
stands near the lake.
    screaming at the bees.

river approaching heaven.
    glamorous yellow aspens.
it's snowing in the song.
    soon the empty words.

spread of pine needles.
    wet feet on concrete.
eternity's not a game.
    the seasons are amazing.

sea greenness and the journey.
    dreaming at the gate.
are we in or of the dance?
    a handsome secret man.

the shadow of your smile.
    fracture of your hand.
comparisons are listening.
    blue eyes down the line.

appetite is enough.
    he summarized an owl.
assiduous imperfections.
    snowbank and white towel.

shadow and actor.
    I sat down on the fire.
the plums were overripe.
    the place seemed familiar.

beauty isn't endless.
    thought dies on the tongue.
nothing is transparent.
    everything half done.

what's original now?
    immediate but distant.
naming every gesture.
    history is the vestige.

overflow of powerful grammar.
    waste product: contemplation.
a series of vivid abstractions.
    flourishing off the page.

the god of disproportion.
    moves in fictive time.
a thought on her face.
    submerges once again.

the desperation to mean.
    lucidity and madness.
what does 'ought' propose?
    moral reserves on empty.

the grass is at attention.
    a faucet steadily drips.
the light behind an object.
    needs no complication.

why is Heidegger quiet?
    where's the emperor tonight?
watching with steady eyes.
    nothing thinking something.

Audience in the Dark

Anonymous and silent cinemas
—Christian Metz

The lavishness
and candor

of a sun-
filled house

is one empirical
sculpture

and butter
is another.

•

Intention and
its thing

are being
in the bone.

Disfigurement
and virtue,

for what
that's worth.

•

In the
ontological foundry

the nose on
your face

is perhaps
the best example.

In impressions
of real life,

theorists appear
according to

their size—
detergent for

the laundry
& change for

the Métro.

       •

As the earth
is carried

away on its
tortoise,

a species dwindles
back to

its cat.

•

In time and
in error,

the timid
and the smooth

are all
they ever were.

•

Heroic and cold,
Bill Viola walks

out of a fire,
or between

the fire and sight,
never making

progress, never
growing larger.

       •

When the second
hunger comes,

"God unbecomes"
in the mirror

and the bowl.

       •

What's needed
is a name

for the loss of meaning
between what

is said and what
is understood,

between what
is not

and a knot
in wood.

     •

Sense and madness
of course

are inherent,
but a soul

must be acquired—
"iterations of

a chaotic map."

     •

Excess is
never enough

and once
is not enough,

if chance
is objective.

•

Only pleasure
lasts forever—

the taste of
rain water,

scent of
chandeliers.

•

Bird's eye
view from

chopper two—
below,

a squeaking walk
over black snow.

The urge
to hide nature

in all her
finding places.

•

No, the actual
doesn't count,

not a single
wooden pizza

in a shack
of the realm,

not a game
of the series,

this being that.

•

No time
like the past

to remedy
your fictions,

prepare a
game face.

•

Well, the forest
is the forest,

no going back
on that,

and the corn
is never quiet—

friction in
the aisles.

•

Triumphant
alibis for

a greedy
little war—

the pipeline
is a go

for Unocal
and so …

•

To reeve and
to hold

whatever's in
the plan

like the next
right turn

for a statue
on the town.

•

Where those
from paradise

go on vacation—
over six hills

and into
the essential.

What are those
boats doing

out on
the sound?

•

If the
camera moves

a fiction
is created.

Blur of
a face

on the
perfect elevator.

•

Poetry is
furtive and

that's its
secret. It

likes not
being watched,

like a
voyeur at

the movies.

•

The bolting
of the scene

for other
nearer places.

The language
of a painting

speaks from
the screen where

imaginaries care
what their

vertigos are
reading.

●

The waste product
of movies

is called
contemplation.

The unsleeping
dreamer is

awakened by
each frame.

Elsewhere in
the child,

degree of
acceptance zero.

●

Paul Hoover

Wearing spectacles
to the scene

of undramatic
acts as

something
dries up

or a towel
briefly stiffens.

•

The poetry
of attention

is centered
in absence

and lies
beyond belief.

•

The future lives
entirely in the past,

where the present
whispers to it

something I forget.

•

When the golem
is broken

down to
its clay,

all that's left
is a little

god intention—
midnight skin line

feeling for
its hand.

•

As Poe once said,
more than one mirror
disfigures a room.

•

"Suspicious even
of his admirers"

describes Charlie Parker,
off in the desert

seeking head arrangements—
no quarrel with the music,

excited about his plans.

     •

The world
of examples

is likewise
private.

Norma Desmond
is brought

to light
by the

darkness
in her.

     •

The candor
of objects

depends on
their mood,

lately near panic
and gifted

with tensions.

•

"There is
everything to

speak of,"
Larry Eigner

said, "but
the words

are the
words."

•

Nine miles of road
and not one bump—

misleading easy passage
for a man on the run.

He puts down words
until they gather feeling

and again until they fade.
The moral world resumes.

What pleasure in silence
when the frail gods dance?

●

He had,
it was said,

a talent for
the average:

average life,
average wife.

Even the child
was average.

When some-
thing in him

rebelled one day,
he killed it

very quickly.
It became

his only power;
in this he was

surpassing.

•

Such aphoristic glitter,
the "American quotidian."

We reap from an image
the emblems of desire.

ACKNOWLEDGMENTS

The author is grateful to the editors of the publications in which these poems have appeared:

John Tranter of *Journal of Poetics Research* for "Repetition and Difference," "Unspoken," and "Define: Mother Tongue."

Rebecca Wolff of *Fence* for "The Urgency."

Don Share of *Poetry* for "Darkness of the Subjunctive."

Bradford Morrow of *Conjunctions* for "Written," "Handwritten," "Dead Man Writing," "The Book of Unnamed Things," "The Book of Nothing," "Made to Resemble," and "The Windows (Speech-Lit Islands)."

Jordan Stempleman of *Sprung Formal* for "Why Is Quiet 'Kept'?"

The student editors of *14 Hills* 20.2 (Spring 2014) and Don Selby and Diane Boller of *Poetry Daily* for "First Language."

*

The long poem "Audience in the Dark" was written under the constraint of a single twenty-four hour day using a small Marble Memo notebook of 40 sheets of paper. Each original handwritten page is indicated by an asterisk.

The poem "Written" was inspired by a poem of Wisława Szymborska.

The titles of the poems "Define: Mother Tongue" and "Define: Contemplation" were influenced by Andrew Joron's work, "Define Lion."

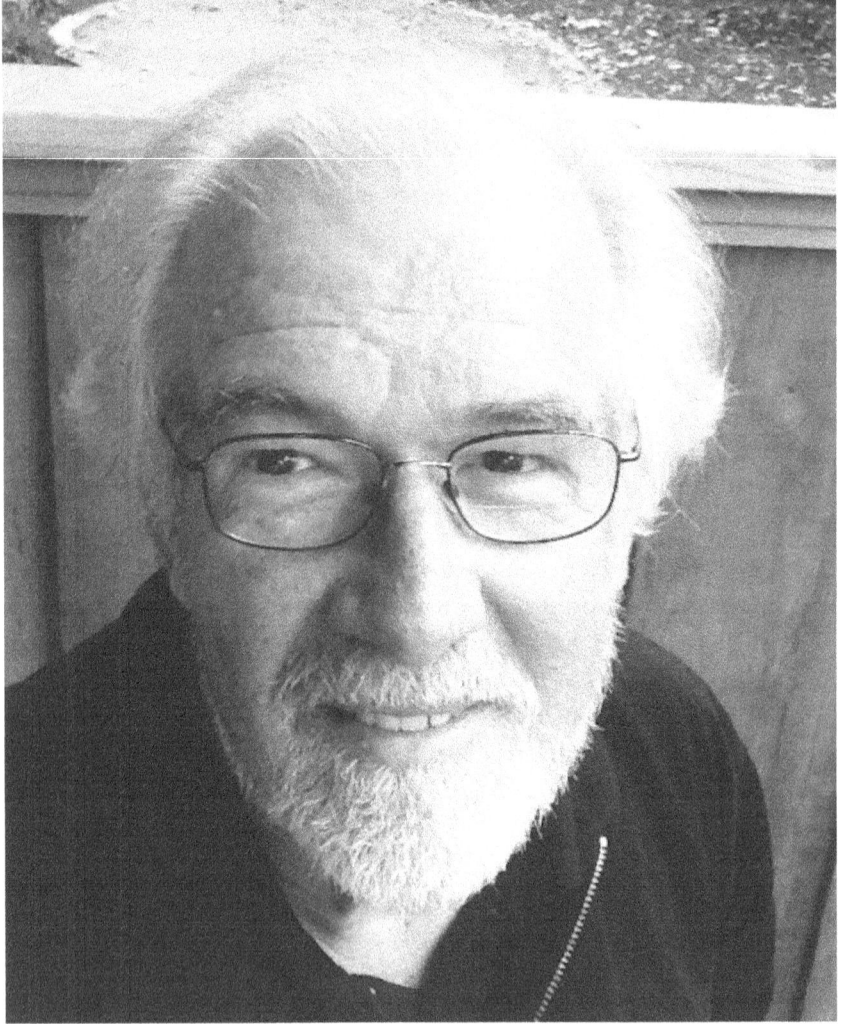

ABOUT THE AUTHOR

PAUL HOOVER was born in Harrisonburg, Virginia, in 1946. He served as a conscientious objector during the Vietnam War, an experience recounted in his novel, *Saigon, Illinois,* published by Vintage Contemporaries. For many years, he taught at Columbia College Chicago, where he founded *Columbia Poetry Review.* He also helped to establish The Poetry Center at School of the Art Institute, an important reading series. With Maxine Chernoff, he edited and translated the *Selected Poems of Friedrich Hölderlin,* for which they received the PEN-USA Translation Award. They also edited the well-known literary magazine, *New American Writing.* With the Mexican poet María Baranda, he edited and translated *The Complete Poems of San Juan de la Cruz.* Editor of *Postmodern American Poetry: A Norton Anthology* (1994 / 2013), he is a Professor of Creative Writing at San Francisco State University. Recipient of numerous literary awards including an NEA Fellowship, the Frederick Bock Award of Poetry, and the Jerome J. Shestack Prize of *American Poetry Review,* he lives in Mill Valley, California.

PREVIOUS WORKS

Poetry

The Windows (Argotist E-books, 2013)

Desolation: Souvenir (Omnidawn, 2012)

Sonnet 56 (Les Figues Press, 2009)

Edge and Fold (Apogee Press, 2006)

Poems in Spanish (Omnidawn Press, 2005)

Winter (Mirror), Flood Editions, 2002

Rehearsal in Black (Salt Publications, 2001)

Totem and Shadow: New & Selected Poems (Talisman House, 1999)

Viridian (University of Georgia Press, 1997)

The Novel: A Poem (New Directions, 1990)

Idea (The Figures, 1987)

Nervous Songs (L'Epervier Press, 1986)

Somebody Talks a Lot (The Yellow Press, 1983)

Letter to Einstein Beginning Dear Albert (The Yellow Press, 1979)

Fiction

Saigon, Illinois (Vintage Contemporaries, 1988)

Essays

Fables of Representation (University of Michigan Press, 2004)

Publications Edited

Postmodern American Poetry: A Norton Anthology, 2ⁿᵈ Edition (1994, 2013)

New American Writing (literary magazine), 1986 to present

www.ingramcontent.com/pod-product-compliance
Lightning Source LLC
Chambersburg PA
CBHW022144090426
42742CB00010B/1380